Using a Magnet

SUPER SCIENCE TOOLS

Adrienne Beaucage

LIGHTBOX
openlightbox.com

LIGHTBOX

Go to **www.openlightbox.com** and enter this book's unique code.

ACCESS CODE

LBXC6833

Lightbox is an all-inclusive digital solution for the teaching and learning of curriculum topics in an original, groundbreaking way. Lightbox is based on National Curriculum Standards.

LIGHTBOX SUPPLEMENTARY RESOURCES

SHARE Share titles within your Learning Management System (LMS) or Library Circulation System

CURRICULUM Find national and state curriculum correlations

CITATION Create bibliographical references following APA, CMOS, and MLA styles

STANDARD FEATURES OF LIGHTBOX

AUDIO High-quality narration using text-to-speech system

ACTIVITIES Printable PDFs that can be emailed and graded

SLIDESHOWS Pictorial overviews of key concepts

VIDEOS Embedded high-definition video clips

WEBLINKS Curated links to external, child-safe resources

TRANSPARENCIES Step-by-step layering of maps, diagrams, charts, and timelines

INTERACTIVE MAPS Interactive maps and aerial satellite imagery

QUIZZES Ten multiple-choice questions that are automatically graded and emailed for teacher assessment

KEY WORDS Matching key concepts to their definitions

This title is part of our Lightbox digital subscription

Lightbox Grades 3–5 Subscription
ISBN 978-1-5105-5424-5

Access hundreds of Lightbox titles with our digital subscription. Sign up for a **FREE** subscription trial at **www.openlightbox.com/trial**

The digital components of this book are guaranteed to stay active for at least five years from the date of publication.

Using a Magnet

SUPER SCIENCE TOOLS

CONTENTS

A FORCE OF NATURE

Scientists use special tools to explore the world around them. They use these tools to conduct **experiments**. Tools also help people with **observation**.

Magnets are one kind of tool used for science. A magnet is a rock or piece of metal that creates a magnetic field. This is an invisible field that causes magnets to pull certain types of metal toward themselves.

Magnets can be small or large. The magnets in a school's science lab are usually small enough to hold in one hand. Other magnets are incredibly large. For example, Earth itself is a magnet. Its magnetic field extends more than 40,000 miles (64,000 kilometers) from the planet's surface.

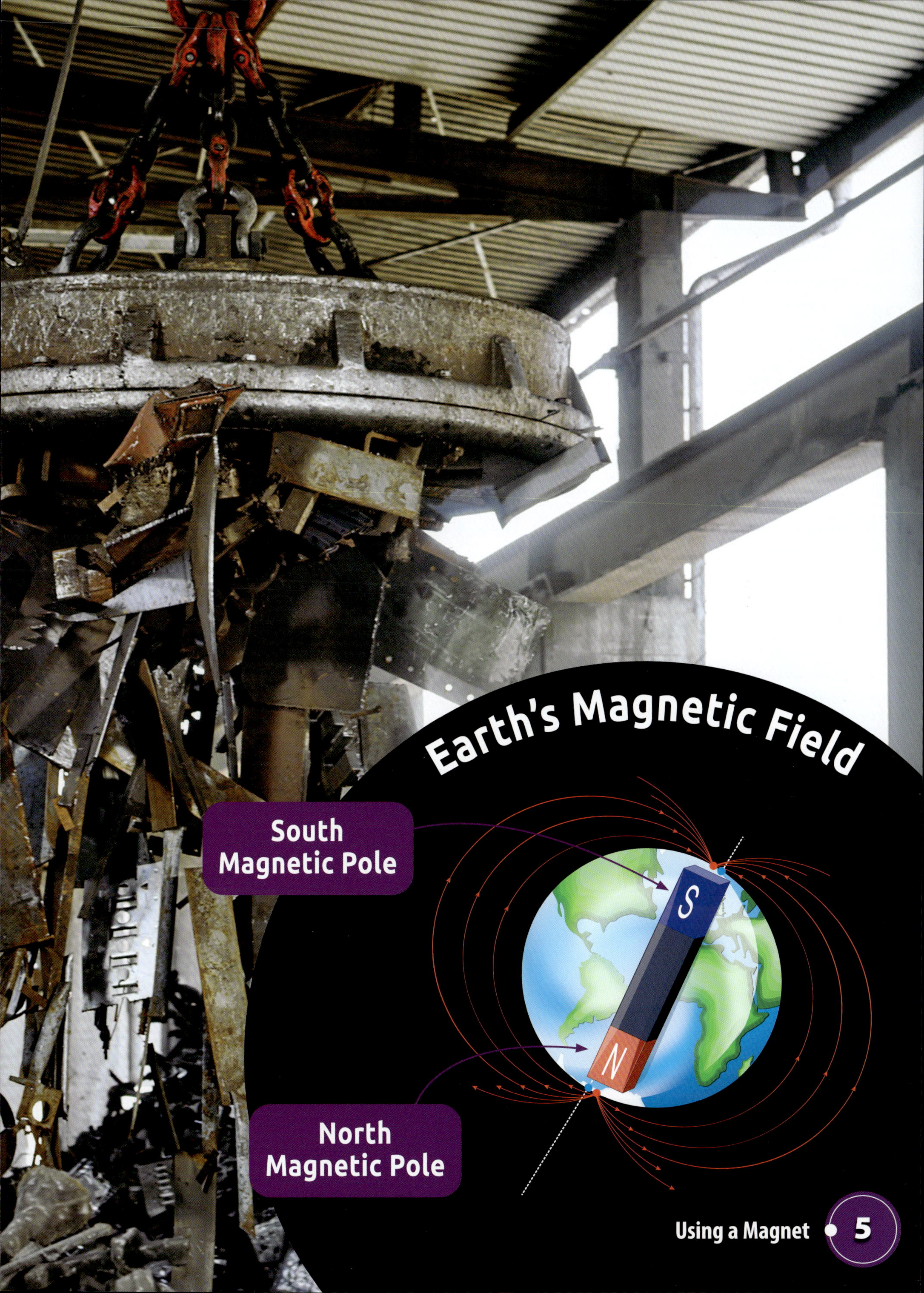
Earth's Magnetic Field
South Magnetic Pole
S
N
North Magnetic Pole

HISTORY OF MAGNETS

The effects of magnets were first observed more than 2,000 years ago. The ancient Greeks are known to have used a **mineral** called lodestone. It would **attract** other pieces of the same mineral. The ancient Greeks called it a magnet.

William Gilbert is often called the "father of magnetism."

Magnets have been used for scientific purposes since the 1500s. An English scientist named William Gilbert was the first person to study magnets using the scientific method. Soon after, other scientists did experiments with magnets and learned more about their fields. Human understanding of magnetism increased greatly in the 1900s. This led to the development of new technologies. Today, much of what people know about magnets comes from the work of two 20th century German scientists, Werner Heisenberg and Ernst Ising.

Magnets Timeline

1600
William Gilbert experiments with magnets and finds that Earth itself is a magnet.

1820
A scientist named Hans Christian Oersted learns how magnetism and electricity are connected.

1945
Engineer Percy Spencer invents the microwave oven, which uses electric and magnetic fields to heat food.

Today
Magnets are used in renewable energy technologies, electric motors, medical **equipment**, and more. New and exciting potential uses for magnets continue to be discovered.

PARTS OF A MAGNET

A magnet has two ends called poles. One end is the north pole, and the other end is the south pole. The magnetic force of a magnet flows from the north pole to the south pole, creating a magnetic field around the magnet. A line called the magnetic axis joins the north and south poles.

When two magnets come into contact, the north pole of one magnet attracts the south pole of the other. However, two north poles or two south poles **repel** each other. This is because similar poles repel one another, while opposite poles attract.

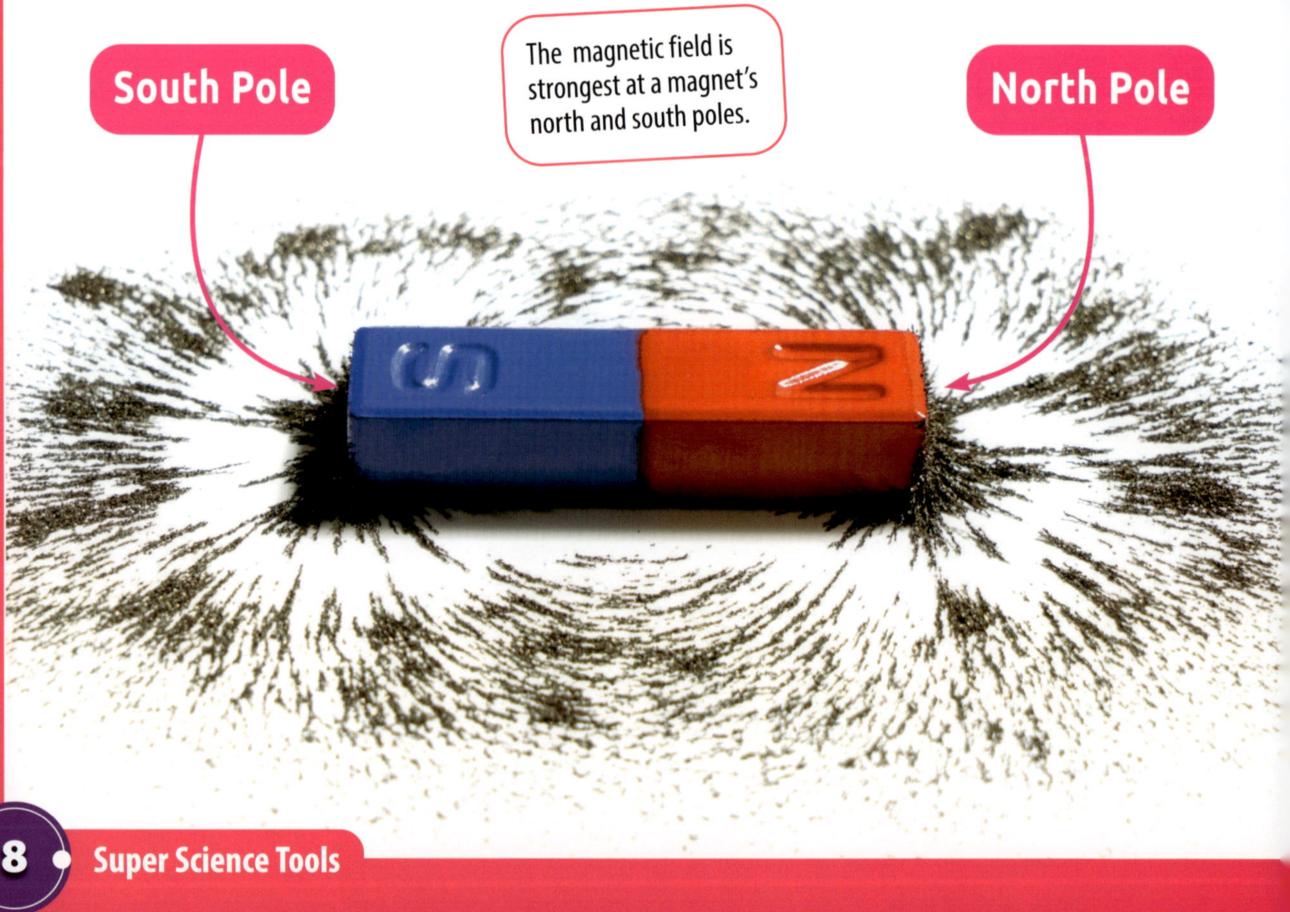

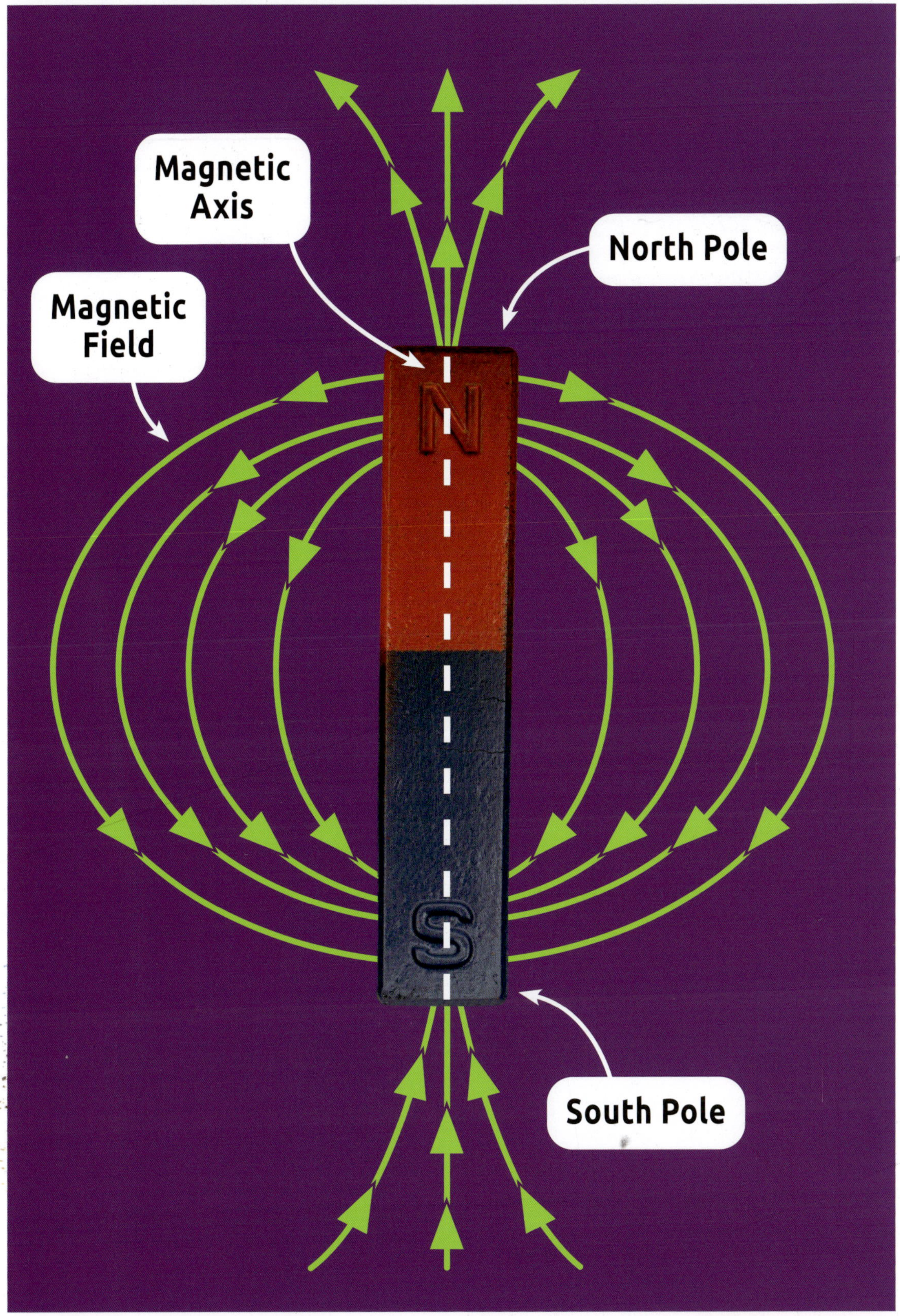
Magnetic Axis
North Pole
Magnetic Field
N
S
South Pole

Magnets should always be handled carefully. Even small magnets can be very strong, so it is important to use them properly.

HOW IT WORKS

Everything in the universe is made up of very small units known as atoms. An atom has a core called the nucleus in its middle. Tiny **particles** called **electrons** spin around the nucleus. These electrons carry an electric charge. As electrons move, their electric charge creates a magnetic field.

In **ferromagnetic** metals, such as iron, nickel, and cobalt, the tiny magnetic fields from the electrons in their atoms add up. This makes the metals magnetic. These metals are attracted to magnets, but are not magnets themselves. They can be changed into magnets by electricity or by magnets.

Magnets and magnetic materials are everywhere. In addition to the magnets scientists use in labs, there are magnets in objects that people use every day. Many people use magnets to attach pictures or notes to their refrigerators. Common objects such as fans, washing machines, cars, and even some trains use magnets to work.

Maglev trains are trains powered by magnets. Japan is building maglev bullet trains that could become some of the fastest trains in the world.

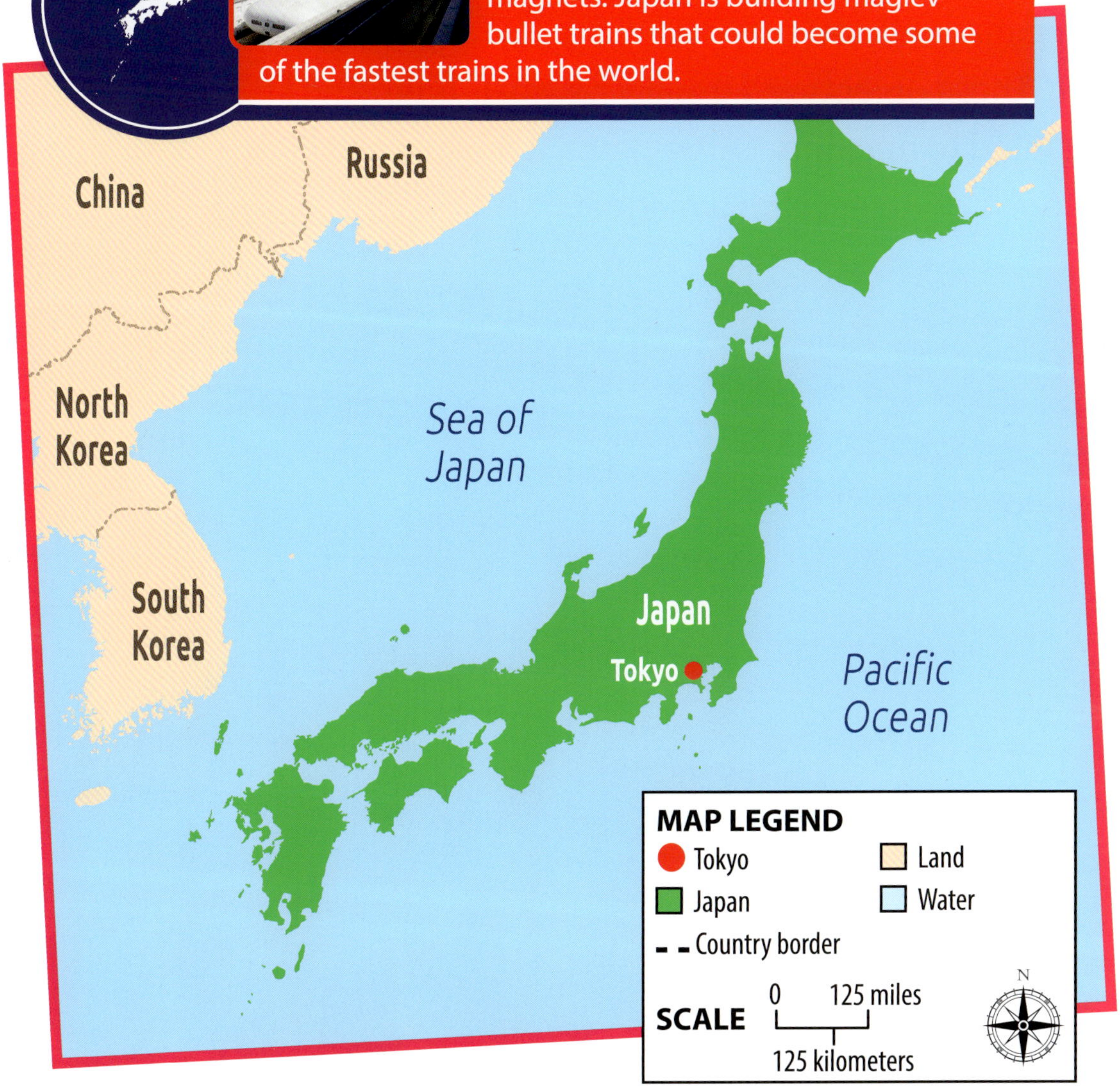

USING A MAGNET

To use a small metal magnet, such as a bar or **horseshoe magnet**, pick it up and hold it close to an object. A non-magnetic object, such as a pencil or piece of paper, will not react. However, magnetic objects will be attracted to the magnet. Nails and some coins are examples of magnetic objects.

Some magnetic objects may move toward a magnet on their own. These objects will usually be small, light, and strongly attracted to magnets. Other times, it may be necessary to touch an object with a magnet.

A horseshoe magnet's shape makes it more powerful than a bar magnet of a similar size.

Magnets can also be used to pick up other magnets. Remember to touch the north pole of one magnet to the south pole of the other, or else it will be repelled instead.

Since magnetic tiles are attracted to each other, they can be used to build more stable structures than building blocks.

Magnetic Attraction

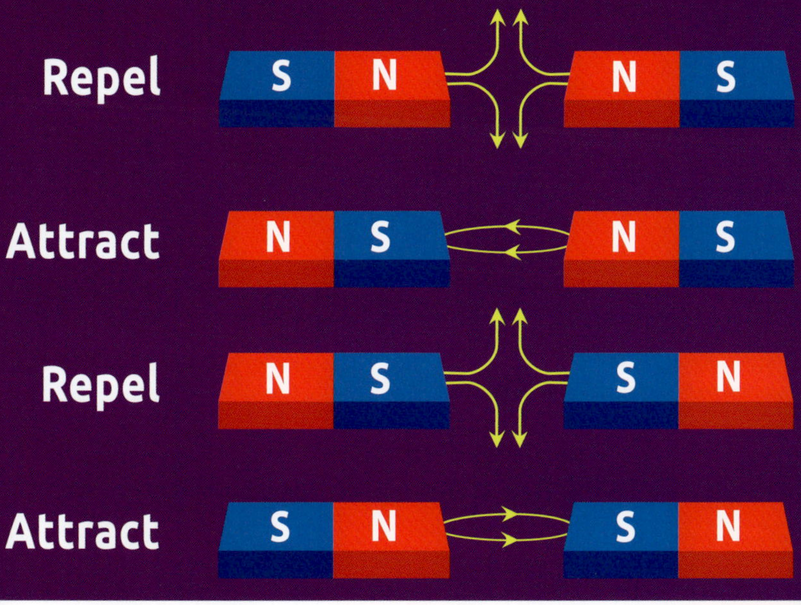

THE SCIENTIFIC METHOD

The scientific method helps people understand how the world works. Scientists use it as a way to answer questions. The method involves testing a hypothesis with an experiment.

1 QUESTION

Ask a question about something that you want to learn more about.

2 RESEARCH

Gather information about the topic. You can use books or the internet to do research.

3 HYPOTHESIS

Based on your research, write down what you think the answer to your question will be. This is your hypothesis.

4

EXPERIMENT

Design an experiment to test your hypothesis. Then, gather the materials you need and perform the experiment.

5

OBSERVATION

Observe your experiment and write down what happens.

6

ANALYSIS

Analyze your observations. Can you figure out what happened and why? This is called cause and effect. The cause is the reason something happened. The effect is what happened.

7

CONCLUSION

Based on your experiment and analysis, was your hypothesis correct? Write down your results and share what you learned with others.

EXPERIMENT

IS IT MAGNETIC?

Cassie is a young scientist. She is learning about magnets in school. Her teacher holds up a crayon, a paper clip, and an eraser. He asks Cassie's class if these objects are magnetic. Cassie thinks she knows the answer. Can she use science to prove it?

1. QUESTION Are crayons, paper clips, and erasers magnetic?

2. RESEARCH Cassie goes to her library and finds a book about magnets. She learns that some metal objects are magnetic. Cassie's school librarian helps her to research online, and she discovers that paper clips are usually made of metal. Cassie also learns that crayons are usually made of wax, while erasers are typically rubber. Based on her research, Cassie believes that only the paper clip is magnetic.

3. HYPOTHESIS The paper clip is magnetic, but the crayon and eraser are not.

4. EXPERIMENT Cassie uses a U-shaped magnet for her experiment. She places each of the objects on the desk in front of her. They are spaced far apart. One at a time, she slowly touches each object with the magnet.

5. OBSERVATION The crayon and eraser do not move when they are touched by the magnet. However, the paper clip sticks to the magnet when touched.

6. ANALYSIS The magnet generates an invisible force that attracts the metal paper clip. The effect caused by this field is the paper clip sticking to the magnet.

7. CONCLUSION The experiment supports Cassie's hypothesis. The paper clip is magnetic. The crayon and eraser are not.

EXPERIMENT

MAGNETS UNDERWATER

Have you ever clapped your hands underwater? Try clapping your hands in a swimming pool or bathtub. It is much harder than clapping your hands in the air. Jim wonders if water also makes it harder for a magnet to work. What can he learn using the scientific method?

1. QUESTION Does water impact how well a magnet works?

2. RESEARCH Jim knows that water is a liquid. He also knows that air is a gas. He uses the internet to research liquids and gases. Jim learns that particles in a liquid are close together, while particles in a gas are farther apart. He thinks the close particles in water may reduce the strength of a magnet's magnetic force.

3. HYPOTHESIS A magnet will have less force when used underwater.

4. EXPERIMENT Jim places a plastic ruler on a table and puts a metal paper clip beside it. He slowly slides a magnet along the ruler, moving closer to the magnet. The magnet attracts the paper clip when they are 2 inches (5 centimeters) apart. Then, Jim fills a plastic tub with water and repeats the same steps. This time, the ruler, magnet, and paper clip are underwater.

5. OBSERVATION Jim observes that the magnet attracts the paper clip underwater when they are 2 inches (5 cm) apart.

6. ANALYSIS Jim's experiment had the same results in the air and underwater. The water did not have any effect on the magnet's force.

7. CONCLUSION The experiment **disproves** the hypothesis. Water does not impact the force of a magnet.

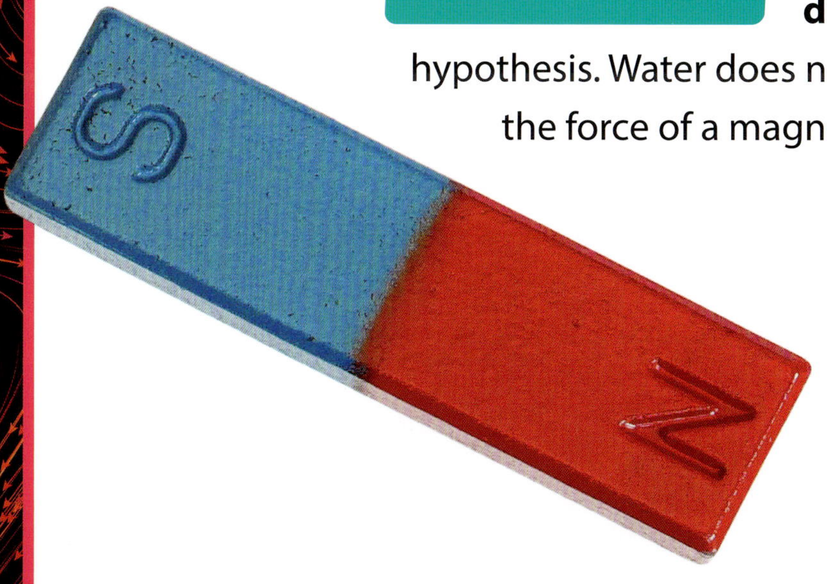

ACTIVITY

CREATE A COMPASS

A compass is a tool used to determine direction. It has a magnetic needle that points to Earth's **North Pole**. This means that a compass always points north. Follow these steps to create your own compass.

MATERIALS

- Bowl of water
- Bar magnet
- Metal sewing needle
- Red marker
- Sheet of wax paper
- Tape
- Scissors
- Compass

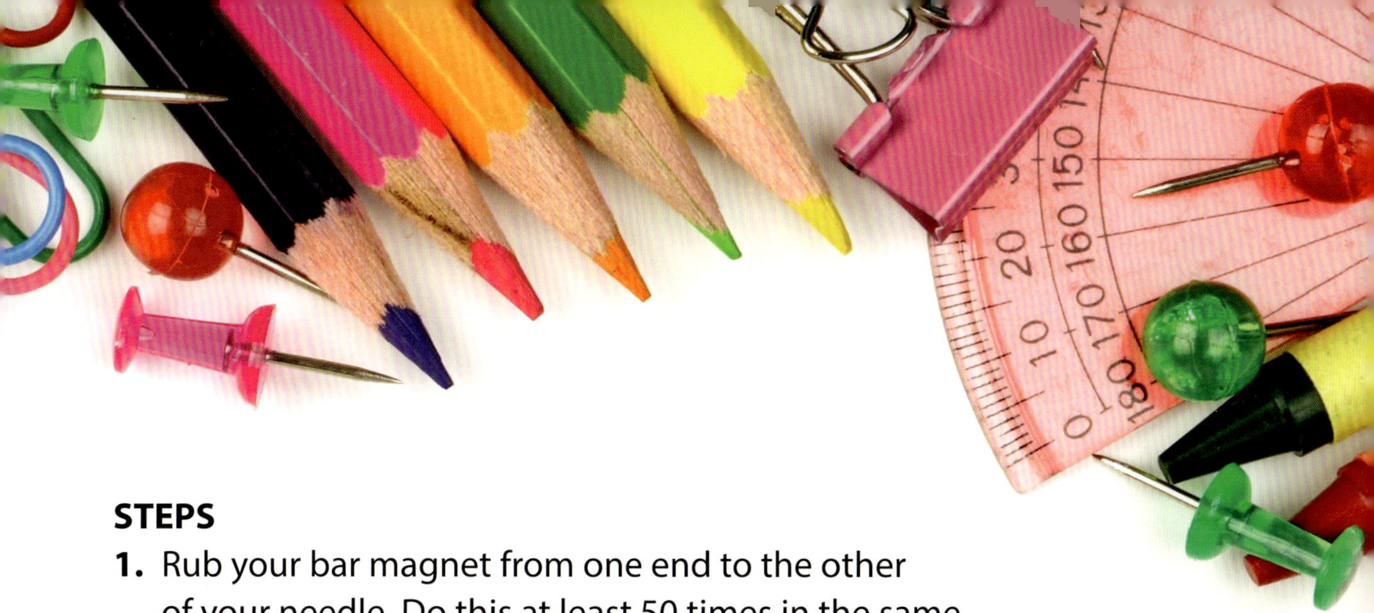

STEPS

1. Rub your bar magnet from one end to the other of your needle. Do this at least 50 times in the same direction.

2. Use your marker to color half the needle red.

3. Cut the wax paper into a circle with a 1 inch (2.5 cm) **diameter**. Tape the needle to the center of the circle.

4. Set the bowl of water on a flat surface, such as a desk.

5. Carefully place the wax paper and needle so that they float on the surface of the water. The needle should be on the top side of the wax paper.

6. Watch what happens to the needle. Does it spin? What direction is the red end of the needle pointing toward? Compare this to a real compass to discover whether the red end is pointing north or south.

MAGNET QUIZ

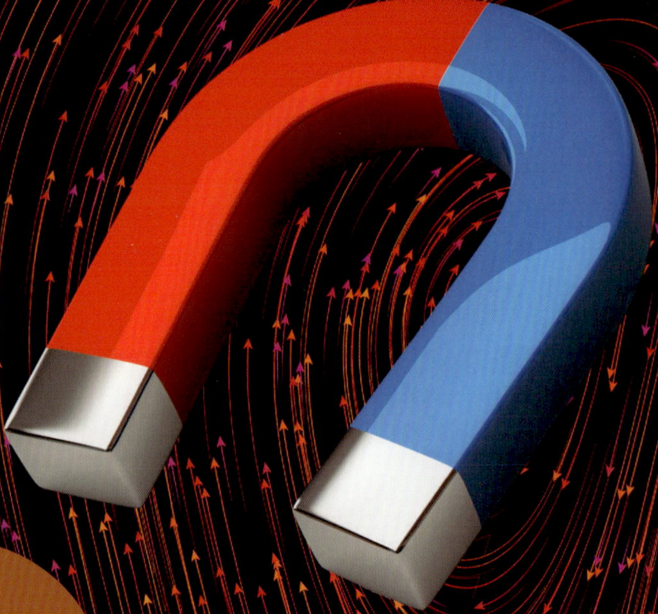

1
How far does Earth's magnetic field extend?

2
What magnetic mineral did the ancient Greeks use?

3
Who first researched magnets using the scientific method?

4
What makes a horseshoe magnet more powerful than a bar magnet of a similar size?

5
How many poles does a magnet have?

6
Do similar poles attract or repel one another?

7
What are trains powered by magnets called?

8
How can some metals be changed into magnets?

9
Who invented the microwave oven?

10
Is a crayon magnetic?

Answers:
1. More than 40,000 miles (64,000 km) from Earth's surface **2.** Lodestone **3.** William Gilbert
4. Its shape **5.** Two **6.** Repel one another **7.** Maglev trains **8.** By electricity or by magnets
9. Percy Spencer **10.** No

KEY WORDS

attract: pull toward

diameter: distance across a circle through its center

disproves: shows that something is false

electrons: small, negatively charged particles in an atom

equipment: items needed for a particular activity

experiments: scientific procedures performed to discover something

ferromagnetic: materials that can be permanently changed into magnets

horseshoe magnet: U-shaped permanent magnet

mineral: a solid, non-living substance found in nature

North Pole: the magnetic south pole near the northernmost point on Earth's surface

observation: watching and noticing what happens

particles: small pieces of matter

repel: push away

INDEX

LIGHTBOX

SUPPLEMENTARY RESOURCES

Click on the plus icon found in the bottom left corner of each spread to open additional teacher resources.

- Download and print the book's quizzes and activities
- Access curriculum correlations
- Explore additional web applications that enhance the Lightbox experience

LIGHTBOX DIGITAL TITLES
Packed full of integrated media

VIDEOS

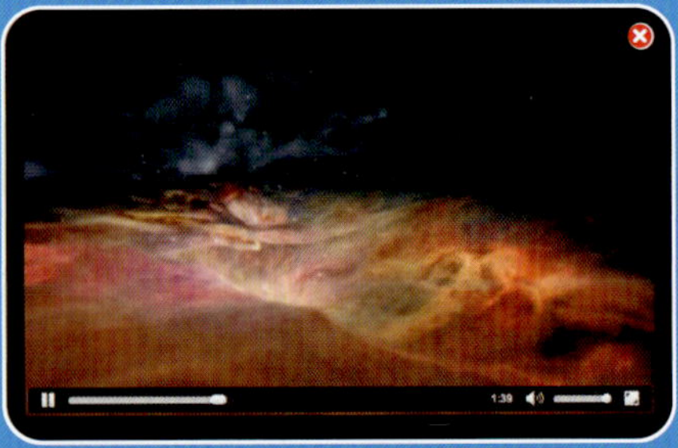

INTERACTIVE MAPS

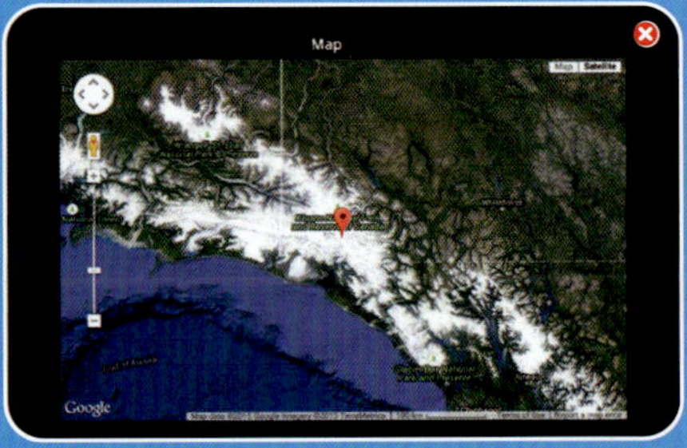

WEBLINKS

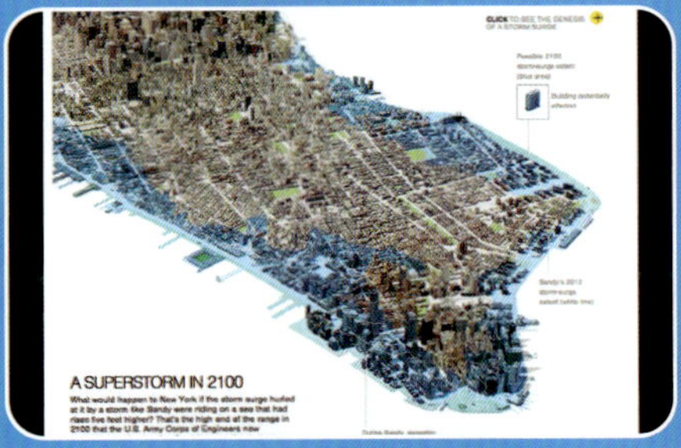

SLIDESHOWS

QUIZZES

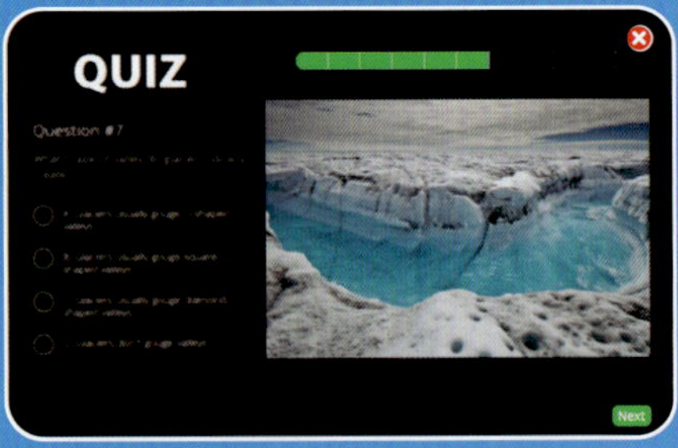

OPTIMIZED FOR
- ✔ TABLETS
- ✔ WHITEBOARDS
- ✔ COMPUTERS
- ✔ AND MUCH MORE!

Published by Lightbox Learning Inc.
276 5th Avenue, Suite 704 #917
New York, NY 10001
Website: www.openlightbox.com

Library of Congress Control Number: 2024936116

ISBN 978-1-5105-5917-2 (hardcover)
ISBN 978-1-5105-5918-9 (static multi-user eBook)
ISBN 978-1-5105-7925-5 (interactive multi-user eBook)

082024
111023

Printed in Guangzhou, China
1 2 3 4 5 6 7 8 9 0 28 27 26 25 24

Project Coordinator: Priyanka Das
Art Director: Terry Paulhus
Layout: Jean Faye Rodriguez

Every reasonable effort has been made to trace ownership and to obtain permission to reprint copyright material. The publisher would be pleased to have any errors or omissions brought to its attention so that they may be corrected in subsequent printings.

The publisher acknowledges Alamy, Getty Images, Shutterstock, and Wikimedia as its primary image suppliers for this title.